Troika

TROIKA

Poems by

Edward Lowbury

John Press

Michael Riviere

NORFOLK · DAEDALUS PRESS · 1977

ISBN 0 9500015 4 6

Printed and Made in Great Britain

Acknowledgments

Acknowledgments are due to the editors of the following periodicals, in which most of these poems first appeared: Birmingham Post, Dart, Eastern Daily Press, Encounter, Image, Listener, New Statesman, New York Times, New Poetry, Outposts, Penguin New Writing, Poetry Quarterly, Poetry Review, Review of English Literature, Sunday Times, Southern Review (Louisiana), Times Literary Supplement, University College Record, Vogue, Wave, Western Mail. 'Ice Storm in Cincinnati' was published in PEN *New Poems,* 1965, and 'The Lily Crucifix, Long Melford' in *The Great Church of the Holy Trinity, Long Melford,* by Edmund Blunden. 'Why won't you let me speak?' was broadcast in *Poetry Now* (BBC 3).

Contents

MICHAEL RIVIERE

Edward Lowbury

The Falls of Iguasu
(for Christopher Lawrence)

To describe the place
Where a mile-wide river, peaceful between
Archaic jungles,
Gradually accelerates, ripples, wriggles among
Savage boulders
And suddenly disappears over an escarpment
Calls for words
Able to shake the earth as the Falls shake it.
But words fall short –
So let me record instead the flight of sleek
Black swifts
Which pierce the descending white water-curtain
To perch on the wet
Rock face, and emerge in twos or threes
Plunging through
The permanent rainbow on the billowing spray:
Again and again
They dive through it, to catch invisible
Midges in mid-air
Or butterflies with wing-span wide enough
To lift a bird,
And (though one-day's-wonder) lovely enough
To last for ever –
The soul's attire . . . Let me record the film
Of spray, fine as smoke,
Through which the Falls plunge, pound – but look

Like apparitions;
The moving sculpture, the lace bouncing upward
From rocks below
In the Devil's Throat – *Garganta do Diabo*;
The silent eyes
Of thunderstruck spectators; the organ
Counterpoint
Of dying falls, a fugue in many voices,
Never once
Repeating itself; and the Oarsman who rows me
Serenely,
With crossed arms, over the still, the accelerating
Waters, across
Ripples, runnels, between savage boulders –
Within yards
Of the overflow, to one harbouring Rock,
The safe place
From which I stare down the cataract
Into the churning
Gorge, eyes and senses dragged down
By the pull of the earth
To follow a falling river – but raised up
As well, against
This trick of gravity to a new awareness
And praise.

The Hawk Moth

Now it was dark in the garden, but indoors
The children went on playing. Suddenly
A black moth came in through the open window
And fluttered hugely against lamps, walls,
Faces; black in wing and body, erratic,
Trying to put out the light, it scared a few
At first; soon they laughed and chased the thing.

But one, the eldest, shrank when it flew near,
Shut eyes, shuddered even to think of it.
She knew the moth was harmless, but that knowledge
Seemed to increase her terror. The others teased her:
'Afraid of that! it couldn't hurt a fly.'
Then, catching it, they held it close to her
And pinned her down, making her scream and struggle.

It seemed she knew the moth was something more
Than wing and body; a sort of emanation
Of something new which fluttered in her breath –
A black angel heralding the end of childhood,
And bringing word of the strange afterlife
On earth – at once repellent and compelling –
That lay before her after childhood's end.

Metamorphosis I

Changing from the angelic form
Of tadpole – a sort
Of emancipated sperm

That slides, brisk and alert,
Through quiet streams – to this
Homunculus, a cruel sport,

The frog with heavy eyes –
Seems like a downward growth;
Quite opposite, the rise

From groping and uncouth
Caterpillars to winged
Emblems of the soul: beneath

A moon's glare the young are changed
Merely from child to man.
The barrier they infringed

As blown amphibian
Or unhatched butterfly,
Causing aesthetic pain,

Was human vanity, –
The unwillingness to laugh
At our absurdity

When we are taken off.

Metamorphosis II

At sixteen, gives a damn for what might happen
In sixty years; chain-smoking, sees old age
As something foreign to him, like cancer;
Sees cancer as something foreign, like old age.
Inspiring the slow poison, he feels big,
Flaunts his virility,
Ready to kick that later, shrunken self –
The sleazy housebreaker – downstairs; roars
With open throttle across the red lights;
And goes on feeling, as the years inch forward,
The same scorn for the old tortoise lurking
Somewhere ahead in that unthinkable future;
Goes on feeling the same, thinking the same,
Turning the undipped light of his virility
On passing eyes – till one day, entering
His own house, he takes the force of a boot
Square in the chest, and topples backward; hears
A voice, that might have been his own, blurt
'Get out, old tortoise, thief, housebreaker!'
Short of breath, paralysed, can't make out
What change has come, and who stands smirking there
At the top of the stairs, making himself at home.

The Typewriter
(For Vivienne Young)

'So now you have been told:
I or my breakfast may grow cold'
from *A Prospect of Death,* by Andrew Young

The sound I'd least expect to hear
    In the small hours from the box room
        At the top of the house – a virtuoso
Performance on a typewriter!

We all heard it. All three
    Heard it again the next night –
        And dashed, this time, to have a look,
But found the room dark and empty.

There in a corner, true enough,
    Stood the old Remington on which
        Our grandfather, Thomas Old,
Had typed his books. The lid was off.

The year he died just such a clatter
    Filled the house, while typed sheets
        Of his own 'Life' slid to the floor,
Leaves for the next gale to scatter.

He swept the lot under his bed,
    Unfinished . . . glancing now
        At the carefree script, we see
How much he must have left unsaid.

Then last night into my ears
　　The sound of a typewriter again
　　　　Broke through shallow walls of sleep;
I jumped from bed and rushed upstairs

To the box room: under the door
　　A line of light was showing. Still
　　　　The frantic clatter . . . I burst in;
Typed sheets were scattered on the floor.

Not even looking to see who
　　Sat typing there, I scooped the lot;
　　　　Read one short sentence: there it was –
The Life, finished, complete, and new !

I staggered, hugging the strange treasure,
　　Back to my room. Now sudden sleep
　　　　Came over me, and when I woke
To read those pages at my leisure,

To meet the real Thomas Old –
　　The room was bare, the scripts had vanished;
　　　　But one short sentence I had read,
Came back: 'So now you have been told'.

Vicarious

Increasingly, our joys become vicarious;
    Watching a daughter's face light up with wonder
On swings or roundabouts, or turn hilarious
    At a crazy rhyme or a linguistic blunder,
We come to require unseasonable devices;
    Can't pass a funfair; revel in the ferment
Of Brighton beach or in the queue for ices
    Or games which till not long ago were torment.
Vicarious, too, our troubles: we detest
    The rain which spoils hopscotch or rounders; mourn
The loss of a doll, death of a fish. The best
    Part of us comes away and is reborn.
And if a child runs off, in the dark frost
We find it is ourselves that we have lost.

THREE REFLECTIONS

I *While in Rome*

Your word of praise for foreign parts – quite rare –
Was that you felt at home while you were there;
But why this make-believe that you're back home
In Birmingham while, briefly, you're in Rome?

II *Apartheid Theology*

Two worlds – one black, one white; and to receive
    Souls of their own colour, two heavens exist;
But must we, to make sense of it, believe
    In two gods, or in one grey Dualist?

III *Manhattan*

Look up at times – not too conspicuously
    In case you're called the tourist that you are –
And see the Babel of this vacant sky,
    Each window twinkling like a giant star;

The pinnacles that catch the early light
    And Towers of Mammon that entice the eye
To a more rarefied and brazen height
    Than any spire which whispers 'deity'.

Second Childhood

Not so bad for some, when long sight
    Obliterates the middle ground of memory.
Forgetting what we told her yesterday,
  She asks the same question
  And hears the same news –
For the first time again,
    With the same transport of discovery.

The sun seems no more than a full moon
    To enfeebled eyes; but stars shine through
At the height of day – discovered memories
  Of childhood, not noticed
  Through years when the blaze
Of day blotted out
    Things far from the daily round, the immediate view.

Looking out of the window now, she sees
    A landscape known since first she came this way
Long years ago, and finds it unfamiliar,
  Like a new country; and though
  The days are blurred, and each
Is like the rest, –
    None leaves much trace, each is the First Day.

Her earth revolves no longer round the Sun,
    Rotates no more on its own axis: flat
And fixed, it now accepts without question

The moon to nurse her
By night, the sun by day. –
While others rush and fret
      Around her, she does nothing and is glad.

In the family circle she alone looks out
      From tearless and unclouded eyes. All strife
Forgotten now, she radiates contentment,
   Unbothered by lost powers
   While she's allowed her special cup;
Not noticing the loss of grey
      Matter which others take for loss of life.

The Message of Christmas Island*

The Dinosaur which feared no enemy
    And never saw the need to fly or think
Died out, leaving the world to smaller fry –
    Tusker and lizard, leopard, missing link.

At home – in the nursery – a frog aping a bull
    Exploded, trying to impress her young;
Again the world was left more beautiful
    For the loss of a swelled head and a bloated tongue.

Now Man, determined not to be outshone
    By such forerunners, threatens to bring down
Roof, walls and world not on himself alone
    But on whatever lives, handing the crown

Back to his Maker, who may now repent
Some trivial flaw in the Experiment.

* Testing ground of a British nuclear device

Hail Holy Light
(for Joan Penman)

'Do you see that lime tree,
A blaze of green light, but gashed
By lightning in the storm last week?'
I said I saw no tree like that.
'You will' she said; and almost
Before the words were out, as we walked on,
There it was; she saw it first,
Before it emerged from the other side of the barn,
Lit by the June sun
And so much like her picture of it,
I gasped, remembering she was blind.
She reached out and touched a leaf – no groping,
No grasping; it was as though a second sight
Made up for the blank retina.
Serene, and unaware
Of her own beauty, she looked always outwards,
The second sight blind to mirrors.

Back in the house, where others, also blind,
Gathered for supper,
We sat, as darkness fell,
And filled with living words
The spaces from which daylight leaked away.
There was a lamp, but no one thought to light it:
They were their own lamps,
And when we rose

I groped, but they moved lightly, seeing their way
In a darkness where I was blind.

The next day they remembered
My disability; and though
Horizontal beams were blazing through the room
Where we again assembled,
For my sake they switched on the light
Which they would never need.

Discovering an Island

Discovering an island
    Of blindness in one eye,
He saw at once what most
    Can't see before they die –

The audacity of Spring
    Shot through with light that came
Not from the sun, but from
    Some living inner flame;

A threat of blindness cured
    His blindness; but how long
Could this new vision last? –
    Or was the whisper wrong

Which told him such an island
    Without views must grow
To be a continent
    Filling both eyes? – And so

He clasped the miracle
    Of his discovered sight,
But saw approaching blindness
    Like a black parasite –

Till walking, in a trance,
    Down the forlorn track
Of a disused branch line
    He felt the past rush back;

Saw steam trains that used
  To make his childhood's day –
Though in his heart he knew
  No train could come that way;

Looked hard enough to see
  The islands of the blest
Or his dead ancestors –
  And knew he was possessed;

For when he shut his eyes
  Those visions did not fade,
But filled with inner light
  The slowly gathering shade:

His sight must fail, and yet
  He found one needs no eye
To see what most can't hope
  To see before they die.

Why won't you let me speak?

Such vigour at eighty! He – emeritus,
    But with the enquiring zeal
    Of a bright freshman, plus the depth
And tolerance of years; she, garrulous,
His prop, companion, foil, – competitor
    For talking time: if once
    He held the floor, she would chip in
'Why won't you let me speak?' It was a war
Of sorts – and yet a love-match as well,
    For he, the polymath,
    Admired her humour, intellect,
Though what she said seemed mostly trivial.

And then, one day she phoned – not the cascade
    Of usual gossip; just
    'He is dead.' I rushed over to help
And found him sitting there, as she had said,
'So fast asleep, he had lost the urge to breathe.'
    I gasped – the shock due more
    To sensing his live presence than
To the knowledge of his death . . . sitting beneath
His favourite picture, in the 'emeritus' chair
    Good friends had given him
    When he retired; so much at peace,
He needed nothing now, not even air;
And she, the widow (how absurd that sounded!)
    Would let no-one disturb

His meditation; but because
He had always liked, at work, to be surrounded
By friends or relatives, she asked them in
 To see how much at peace
 He must have been: 'no, not the end –
This seems more like a phase due to begin . . .'

We sat with him; held teacups, half prepared
 To hear him start 'Where's mine?'
 But she with no competitor
For talking time, talked on; then turned, and stared
Uneasily at his expression; 'Strange,'
 She frowned; 'it's not as calm
 As yesterday; I did not think,
Seeing him then, there could be such a change.'
Yet surely, as I glanced, I caught a streak
 Of the old humour – the words
 About to break out of his mouth
Through a quick smile: 'Why won't you let me speak?'

Antenuptial Fornication

A recording angel – or at least
Owner of the best hand for miles around,
A copybook calligraphy with which
He inscribed the Kirk Sessions
In a plump register; his name, John Innes.
Had he fallen dead, there'd have been no-one else
Who could take over, no man who could flourish
A pen worthy to record for the scrutiny
Of man, – fit for the eye of the Almighty
Himself, – in perpetuity,
The sins of god-fearing men, – such
As stealing coals, forgetting
To pay debts, allowing
Brash offspring to defile the kirk yard
With ball games or fights or caterwaulings,
Coming home high and hitting wife or child,
Horse or cat; or even
Being missed from the congregation
On Sabbath. Compearing, and confessing
Such guilt, they were barred
Till duly repentant
From the Lord's house and all favours
Showered so plentifully on the virtuous.
Each sin was lovingly recorded, the Sinner's name
With lavish flowing curves immortalised
In the script of Innes, the Recorder.

And then, 'On the tenth of June
In the year of our Lord one thousand
Eight hundred and sixty three,'
The minutes read, in the same flawless copperplate,
'Compeared John Innes
Confessing that he had been guilty
Of the detestable sin
Of antenuptial fornication,
For which offence he is suspended
From the privileges of our fellowship
Till he do prove himself duly repentant'.
So the flawless hand recorded flaws
Of which, with such gay flourishes and turns,
It seemed to be as far from shame
As from contrition; rather proud, in fact!
For who'd expect
A farmer to take chances,
To let his seed fall upon stony ground?
A childless marriage might well mean starvation.
It might, perhaps, have been a better law
For man and wife to marry on the day
Their first-born was baptised; but, failing that,
It was a perk, of sorts,
To appear, with florid capitals, inscribed
For all time in the Book of Sins, recorded
By his own hand, this tenth day of June . . .

Who knows how many of the virtuous,
Chancing to feast their eyes on that confession,

Having dutifully clicked their tongues, would sigh
With envy, remembering in whose arms
The sinner earned his ghostly reprimand?

John Press

Design

Compassionate, yet apart, the painter stands,
Sketching the vacant faces of the crowd,
The docile efficiency of the soldiers who hammer
Regulation nails into outstretched hands.
His task being not to change but to record
The design of the world where cruelty and fear
Intersect, and flesh is nailed to the cross,
He observes how the huddling women's sombre cloaks
Set off the glitter of a thrusting spear,
How a curving helmet and an uplifted sword
Counterpoise a chariot-wheel's diagonal spokes;
And, glancing upwards, where a figure is skewered,
The limbs contorted, etchings of pain on the face,
A crown of thorns twisted in bloodied tangles,
He notes how, in austere, geometrical grace,
A pattern emerges of scalene triangles.

Norfolk

This is my country: beet stacked on the road,
Flint walls discoloured and cracked by storm and flood.

Pines overshadowing miles of beach; at low-tide
One can walk to where North Sea breakers pound and
ride.

Huge churches every few miles: some show-pieces,
Some rotting, walls damp, pews stippled with birds' faeces.

A climate which does not breed philosophers;
Propitious for cultivated squires and painters,

Learned clergymen in Georgian rectories,
Eccentric canons and queer antiquaries.

A land which has nurtured sailors, livestock breeders,
Refugee Huguenot and Flemish weavers.

Not an attractive stock: slow-moving, bleak,
Wary of foreigners, frugal, tough as teak.

Habits alter. Even in the remotest
Villages the telly has ousted incest

As the favourite pastime of a winter's night.
Multiple stores, piped water, electric light,

Decent roads, free secondary education
Have sponged away rural quirks and isolation.

Yet the people remain cautious and taciturn,
Ironsides gone a bit rusty, but still Puritan,

Mistrusting poetry as a waste of time –
Prinking out honest speech with finery and rhyme.

Their rhythm is heavy: boots stamping on clods,
Eyes seldom lifted to the enormous clouds.

I, though long attuned to a different style,
Admiring the baroque, drawn to the volatile,

Haunted by the Mediterranean and Rome,
Stick fast to this clogging soil, and count it my home.

At Sheringham

I stand on the cliff-height;
The sun glitters taper-white
And shoots from the hill cold shafts of piercing light.

A huddled gull
Broods statue-still on a hull:
A wintry kingdom ruled by a feathered numskull.

Frost on the loam
Out-dazzles the sea-foam;
The December landscape is chequer'd and polychrome.

A piebald horse
Canters on the green golf-course;
The cliff-edge is flecked with yellow spurts of gorse.

What looks like peace –
Calm sea, big clouds soft as fleece –
Is only a brief mid-winter armistice.

Hating the fruitful acres,
The warm cities and their makers,
The sea probes the groynes and masses heavy breakers

To filch from the land
What men have plotted and planned,
Till all is razed to shingle on the bare strand.

Grown chilly, I leave
As the shadows bereave
The world of all natural light this Christmas Eve.

Aldeburgh at Christmas

The muffled skaters score the thick ice of the mere,
  The silence is punctured only by the hiss
    Of the keen blades, and the birds' sharp singing
      In the leafless coppice.

Fishermen flip their nets and the sprats tumble down;
  Their silver will tarnish soon on the damp stones;
    Gulls swoop and rip the succulent flesh from
      The filigree bones.

Rushes tipped with frost, sea-mist, a wafer-thin moon,
  A snowy cloud that assumes a dragon's shape:
    Such alchemy transmutes Suffolk meadows
      To a Chinese landscape –

Till English cohorts drive out the foreign devils:
  Goal-posts, a public-house, a rook-crowded birch
    And, on the hill, the square, reassuring
      Tower of the church.

The daffodil-yellow gorse stars a few bushes,
  Street-lamps diffuse golden light as the evening
    Broods on the darkened mere and the bare trees
      Where the sap is rising.

On the Coast of Pembrokeshire

Black cattle crop the rough grass near the cathedral;
Anthem and chime and cry of kittiwake and gull
          Intermingle.

Samphire clusters on the crumbling architraves;
Dewy luxuriant grass smooths over the graves
          Of muted loves.

A tumble-down farm shelters two splintered waggons;
Rampant on the roofless keep, petrified dragons
          Sniff the earth's fragrance.

In the Trappist monastery the silence heals
The world's wounds. Off-shore, the unregenerate seals
          Plunge as the sea swells.

The tree-darkened path savagely twists, plummets. Both
Sea and sun dazzle like road-to-Damascus truth.
          The sands of Amroth

Stretch out nine hard and level miles to Tenby,
Rehearsal-ground for the assault on Normandy.
          The western sky

Is cicatriced now with freshly-bleeding scars.
A broken castle resurrects the massacres
          Of more distant wars.

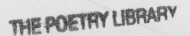

Ice-Storm in Cincinnati

The ice-storm littered roads with red-hot wires,
Robbed homes of water and put out their fires,

To prove the double malice of cold weather
That has the power to burn and freeze together.

Just when their bitterness seemed most intense,
The wind and ice, as though in recompense,

Began to pierce the blackness of the trees
And light the world they had conspired to freeze.

The ice lodged on the boughs in glittering tiers
And hung the darkened sky with chandeliers.

The wind played on the icicles and rime,
Whose frozen music melted to a chime.

Each branch flowered as a symphony in white,
The source at once of music and of light.

But as the sun gathered its strength again
And gently broke the ice-storm's crystal reign,

Though heat and water freshened every house
A barren darkness overwhelmed the boughs.

The frozen spray, whirled into splintered glass,
Spangled with silver jags the soaking grass,

Till the last fragment tumbled slowly down
And the bare branches shrivelled back to brown.

Peach-Tree in the Garden of an Empty House

No blustering winter storm could fell the peach-tree,
But when the fruit grew ripe, a burdened bough
Sagged, and it needed only a faint breeze,
A blue-tit's weight, the swelling of a peach,
And the bough cracked. Five branches brushed the
                                                    ground.
The bark, exposed, at first was soft and creamy,
Stained ochre in the centre. Soon its whorls,
Losing their smell of fresh wood and pulped fruit,
Grew darker, coarser, crusted like a wound.
Marauding boys, scaling the crumbling wall,
Ripped a few juicy peaches, but the rest,
Green, yellow-tinged, suffused with a warm dye,
Some delicately stippled rose-and-peach,
Were pecked and pockmarked by the jabbering birds,
Or dropped and lay discoloured, squelched and foul.
The house was sold; new owners chopped the tree.
Its piled logs saved them half a ton of coal.

Northern Nigerian Chiefs

A dozen visiting Nigerian chiefs,
Tall, stately men in elaborately-woven robes,
Were booked in a country hotel. All had spacious rooms
Overlooking green fields and running streams,
Trees bulging with birds, lilacs puffed out with bloom.
The Chiefs went sailing with the local yacht-club,
Strolled through the fields on warm summer nights
And were stood brandies in the village pub.
When they left, after the usual exchange
Of courtesies, they made a mild complaint.
They wished it had been possible to place them
Somewhere in the bustling centre of Birmingham,
Near the cinemas and Woolworths, where the cars
And buses would have roared cheerfully at them.
They had been most uneasy in the hush
Of the country at night, haunt of strange birds and insects.
They hoped that for the remainder of their programme
They would be housed in some less savage place
And not confined to the heart of the English Bush.

A Victorian Ballad

This was an age of crippled giants,
The prophets denouncing the Gloomy Science,
The artists squeaking a shrill defiance
    In the best Victorian manner.

Kingsley, who started a mild disturbance
With his radical views and Broad Church sermons,
Loathed the French and adored the Germans
    In the best Victorian manner.

When General Eyre in military style
Flogged scores of niggers on a tropical isle
He was dubbed a hero by Thomas Carlyle
    In the best Victorian manner.

Butterfield hated the pagan dome;
He lavished his skill on the Gothic home
And the church made holy with polychrome
    In the best Victorian manner.

Tennyson sweating in the night with fear
Kept the stiff upper lip of a laureate peer
And wrote charades about Guinevere
    In the best Victorian manner.

The models of Rossetti were trained to flex
Their long Pre-Raphaelite goitred necks.
He worshipped Art and doted on Sex
    In the best Victorian manner.

Bareback equestriennes, floggings and wines
Fermented Swinburne's most yeasty lines
Until they knackered him at The Pines
    In the best Victorian manner.

The path descended by way of *Sordello*
To the gemlike flame and the cult of yellow
And Dowson drunk in a plush bordello
    In the best Victorian manner.

Artistic ladies bought the works of Millais,
The Prince dined out with the Jersey Lily
While Oscar languished on bread and skilly
    In the best Victorian manner.

At Sète

In December
We drove from Montpellier through the mountains.
The afternoon sun was still warm, the sky deep blue,
As we descended circuitous roads to sea-level
Then climbed the winding cumbrous streets of the busy
                                                    port,

Enjoying the play of light on the boat-hulls,
The glitter and ripple of light on the sea below.
'It's a pretty tough Communist town', said my companion,
A strange harbour, it seemed, for Paul Valéry to rest in.
At the top of the hill, in a deserted square,
We parked the Deux Chevaux and walked through the
                                                ugly gate

Of the Marine Cemetery (for the long dying fall
Of graveyard by the sea would be false, evoking a lush
Swinburnian garden sprayed by the petalled foam
In langorous summer, or a melancholy waste land
Blanketed by heavy tides as the long ululation
Of the winter north-wester lays its burden on the
                                                darkness).

The concierge told us the way to the grave: take the path
On the left, climb the steps till you come to the cypress.
So we climbed past the black marble slabs, the cracked
                                                    urns,

The moss-covered unconvincing stone angels,
Suddenly, at a sharp right turn we reached the cypress
Marking the family tomb on which was inscribed

The name of Paul Valéry.
It was twilight when we walked back to the parked car,
A flamingo-pink sky stained with blobs of indigo ink
Stretched over the darkening sea, and we shivered with
cold.

It seemed we had paid our tribute and brought away
nothing,

Until, in the sombre, dispiriting asphalt square
Outside the walled boneyard, we paused and listened,
Aware that we shivered partly in joy and because
The wind was rising.

Reading Proust in the Welsh Hills

Grazing a few sheep on the rock-strewn moel,
The shepherd learns the harmonies of the soil.
Swann listens to the sonata of Vinteuil.

Within earshot of the lilting rivulet
Grow wild foxglove, bee-orchis and violet.
Swann gathers the smooth, scented flesh of Odette.

Night falls. The col surrenders to owls and stoats.
Preying on himself, Swann prowls through darkened
streets;
Odette writhes in pleasure between the sheets.

Soft hillside mist shrouds the treacherous ravine;
The blue sea fumes slate-black, clouds grey, glitters green.
Marcel looks into the eyes of Albertine.

Winter beleaguers the shepherd's stone-flagged room,
Ice silvers the bare moel, snowdrifts block the cwm.
Along Swann's Way the hawthorn is always in bloom.

A Diamond for Dylan Thomas

Now
Larks climb,
As   first   light
Melts   the   chill   dew
And their songs' coiled twine
Reels down from the cold dome
Till the skeins ring round the bay.
I   love   the   warm   sun   on   my   bones
But turn from the day's fresh lure and reach
The church humped on the rock where dim saints bled,
And as the choir chant the brave verse of the psalm,
'My heart is fixed, O God, I will sing and give praise',
Cock-crow and dog-bark fade from the far-off farm.
But my heart veers in doubt and mourns the dead
Who once trod taut turf and gull-strewn beach
Then sank to bleared scrawls on dank stones,
Though buds still spurt green, and may
Froths coomb and copse with foam
And the same rays shine
On the dark yew
And the bright
Spring-time
Bough

'Ah, did you once see Shelley plain?'

No, but I twice saw Ezra Pound,
Aged 85, October 1970,
Walking after dinner at da Cici
Along the Fondamenta Cabalà.
I thought that he was making for the Zattere
To look across the lagoon where darkening skies
Had all but blotted out the Redentore;
But he turned left into a narrow *corte*.
I noted his firm step, fine head, bright eyes,
And watched him stride toward home
Like those who in Verona win the prize.

The Shadows

After forty the shadows start to fall.
I think of a few friends
On whom the encroaching darkness descends.

There was one who stared for hours at a wall,
Lying on an iron bed,
With a weight lurching about in his head.

Another, plunging into alcohol,
Found it as bitter as
The lees of sex, the soured wine of the Mass.

A third gulped down fistfuls of seconal
But was still not granted
The long sleep that he had always wanted.

A stomach pump dredged him: a hospital
Passed six shocks through his brain;
A good psychiatrist tried to explain

The root of his trouble was Oedipal.
Though he still cannot sleep
He has some inkling of what makes him weep.

Our own darkness shelters daimons who call
Till we take the long spiral
Down to a stifling, self-created hell.

I too have watched the shadows growing tall.
May light perpetual
Shine on the haunted and redeem us all.

To a Girl with Beehive Hair

At Mycenae the beehive tombs
Are white and cold:
There is no honey in those combs.

Your hair is piled high; it is black,
Lustrous and warm;
It covers your head like a cloak.

Wrap me in your honey-sweetness:
I feel the chill
Of the night, and the hour's lateness.

Soon I shall be deaf to the bees' drone
In my dark cell
Lying still as Agamemnon.

What the Wind Said

White bone clinging to white bone
In their marriage bed,
Haven and shield against menacing weather,
Shivered to hear what the wind said:
'Soon, soon, you must lie alone,
Torn like leaves from an autumn bough,
But till nightfall you may twine together
As you do now.'

White bone resting on white bone
In their common grave,
Safe and sealed against menacing weather,
Were deaf to the comfort the wind gave:
'Nevermore shall you lie alone,
But close as leaves on a summer bough
Till the world's end you may twine together
As you do now.'

Preparations

Silence and sunlight hold the garden poised.
A dozen graduated shades of green
Cohere in muted radiance and are cool.
Too indolent to flicker or to rise,
Trout skulk in the recesses of a pool.
A borzoi stretched beneath a cedar dozes,
Drugged by the sensual harmony of the scene,
As pollen-strained and drowsy butterflies
Cling to the velvet crinkles of the roses.

An old man in a deck-chair turns the page
Of a thick calf-bound folio on his knees,
Then stretches out his hand to reach a rose.
His senses range the landscape and absorb
Nature's profusion checked by human skill:
A clipped yew hedge, smooth turf, exotic trees,
Fields which the Saxons learned to dig and till,
The book he studies and the rose he plucks –
Tokens that man can mitigate the rage,
The brutal energy, of aimless flux.

Can mitigate, but cannot hope to master.
The old man sniffs the roses and recalls
The ceremonious pattern he has made:
Long lunches, boring functions, funerals,
Precise despatches, decorations, braid,
Leaves spent on yachts or shooting on the moors,

A book of memoirs which his friends admired.
All these distractions helped the time fly faster
And dulled the pain of growing old and tired.

For fifty years he observed protocol,
Laid prudent plans for each new embassy;
But how can the most skilled ambassador
School himself for a journey to the dead
Where nobody can ascertain to whom
An envoy ought to be accredited?
He may reflect how trout and cedar tree
And butterfly move peacefully to the fall,
While roses that will grace his darnelled tomb
May ground him in the language of the earth.

After *Le Nozze di Figaro*

It did not last. Before the year was out,
The Count was once again a slave to women,
The Countess had a child by Cherubino,
Susanna was untrue to Figaro,
Young gallants went to bed with Barbarina.
But for a moment, till the music faded,
They all were ravished by a glimpse of heaven,
Where everything is known and yet forgiven,
And all that is not music is pure silence.

The Lily-Crucifix, Long Melford

Engraved in the live centre of the window,
That otherwise is colourless as water,
The stained-glass shines, silver and blue and gold.
As we draw near the gleam assumes a shape:
The lily-petals gradually unfold,
To show, not pistil, stamen or calyx,
Which would have long ago withered and died,
But the unfading emblem of the crucifix,
The deathless body of the crucified.

Michael Riviere

Colditz

I *Oflag Night Piece*

There, where the swifts flicker along the wall
And the last light catches, there in the high schloss
(How the town grows dark) all's made impregnable:
They bless each window with a double cross
Of iron; weave close banks of wire and train
Machine guns down on them; and look – at the first star
Floodlight the startled darkness back again . . .
All for three hundred prisoners of war.
Yet now past them and the watch they keep,
Unheard, invisible, in ones and pairs,
In groups, in companies – alarms are dumb,
A sentry loiters, a blind searchlight stares –
Unchallenged as their memories of home
The vanishing prisoners escape to sleep.

II *New Year in the Cells*

Europe gyved in ice,
Trussed in blood and hunger.

Her abundant warmth and joy
Wastes out of wounds into the snow.

The widow was lucky in the raid
If one child survived.

The ship was lucky at sea
If all drowned soon.

The corpse was lucky in the snow
If he spilt a full guts there.

God curse the cold
That's frozen the bell-tongue;

The war and hunger
That's flayed the ringer;

This starry night,
This starry night.

Seasonal Love

All summer through
The gods of loin and eye
Riotously pursue
The glimpses of her hair and shoulder
In forests from whose startled foliage
Like doves the spiritualities fly.

But when the green
Is scythed away with snow
Only her eyes are seen,
And one God stands declared, to link us
In this transparency of winter
With neighbourly angels to and fro.

From Ronsard

I *'Cependant que ce beau mois dure'*

Let me love you in the sun
Now, while weather holds, Mignonne.
Roses fast as chances die,
And vice versa, so it's said.
Age will dapple that dark head
Soon, almost, as Spring's gone by.

Time's in flower. Field and wood
Prompt this harvest of the blood.
Death, like lovers, has his wish:
Just as – look –we strip again,
Tongue to tongue and vein to vein,
He will strip us of our flesh.

II *A La Forest de Gastine*

I write stretched in your verdurous shade,
    Gâtine, dedicatory
Verses, as Greek poets made
    Their songs to Arcady.
Loved forest, these are lines sent on
    Lest you lack celebration
In days when I, not you, am gone.
    New times, and other nations,
Shall know this leafage of content
    That shields Care off, a whole
Forest the Muses' instrument
    Where, book in hand, I stroll
Lost in those old mythologies
    That – lustful, beautiful –
Glimmer through your green silences.
    Be held inviolable;
Rest happy among the woods of France,
    Numinous, sacred yet
To Muses whom Time and Mischance
    Cruelly disinherit;
Flourish, dim, vast memorial
    That Ronsard celebrated,
Whatever shrines of Europe fall,
    Never deconsecrated.

III *De l'Election de son Sepulcre*

To caves, and to clear springs
Falling in curves and rings,
Counter-point, paradox,
    Through glades, by rocks:

To you, primeval woods,
Heaths, meadows fringed with reeds
Is, anthropomorphic, sent
    My Testament.

When Heaven or Chance or Time
Periods my last rhyme
And puts me out of action
    And out of passion,

Dig for me no rare stone,
Let Carrara alone,
No bust, nothing at all
    On the church wall;

Emphatically no grand
Tomb up the chancel end,
With shields, gilt lettering,
    That kind of thing.

But where my Loir floats by
The Ile Verte let me lie,
Held in that slow stream have
    A natural grave.

There may some river tree
Summer-long shadow me
With murmurous layer on layer
    Of leaf-in-air;

May, thrusting from my ground
To wrap me round and round,
Ivy and honeysuckle
    The place entangle,

And the symbolic vine
Appropriately entwine
One who drew half his mettle
    Out of the bottle.

There, on my festal day,
From near and far away
The shepherds shall converge
    To the stream's edge;

And, innocent office said,
Wine poured and bay leaves shed,
Shall ritually address
    That quiet place:

Green island, happy ground!
Whose verses are renowned
And sung half the world over
    You safely cover

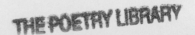

A man who, when alive,
Never had to contrive
Contacts or introductions
    To important persons;

Used no obsequious tricks
On fashionable critics;
Employed no druggery, buggery
    Or skulduggery.

But through these woodlands here
And this Arcadian air
Brought with his life-enhancing
    Lyre, Muses dancing,

Till the calm countryside
Knew his songs far and wide,
Our sheep-walks, glades and pastures
    Graced by his measures.

Stars, let your influence come
To bless that grassy tomb:
Earth, let what from you rises,
    Breeds, fertilises

(Ithyphallic), verdure and water
And warmth, annotate for ever
His text of sensuality
    In sound prosody.

We too, keeping in mind
Fame that he left behind,
Great Pan, will bring him here
    Due praise each year.

Thus, pouring their libation,
With some such recitation
Or coronal of rhyme
    To freshen Time,

Shepherds shall honour me.
But far away I'll be
Then, in vales of Parnassus
    Where cannot reach us

Poets bitter rain
Or snow ever again,
Nothing of this world's weather,
    Hail, or hate either.

Only, the whole year long,
Fruit-blossom and bird-song
And sunshine on green meadows,
    Flowers, leafy shadows,

And winds from summer seas
Idling through plane trees
And myrtles like a river
    That goes on for ever.

Free there, once and for all,
From Leader and General
Who ruin Earth the better
  To prostitute her,

Like brothers born, instead,
We Life-creating Dead
Perfect those skills with which
  We made Earth rich:

Sappho, fished from the sea
Into eternity;
Marlowe called from backgammon,
  Herbert from Heaven . . .

The Muse alone can cure
Sad hearts of this world's care,
And flatter the failing spirit
  With dreams to inherit.

IV '*Ma douce jouvence est passée*'

Youth's gone, so what remains?
    Black teeth, white head, diminished
Forces. Watered veins
    For blood. Cold body. Finished.

Goodbye girls. Goodbye Muse.
    There heart and soul once fed.
Old joys all in disuse
    But fire, and wine, and bed.

Faintness, ennui, worry,
    Short wits and shorter breath,
And for mate now – dawdle or hurry –
    Unfashionable Death;

Whose door is easy enough
    To push through, so they say;
But neither Verse nor Love
    Turns it the other way.

Urbino

Vignette of Duke Federigo

The strength of hope now that of achievement, he still
                              rides out
Early these summer mornings with a few friends (their
                              horses
Led up a vaulted ramp from cool half-underground
                              stables),
The mature man, proven and vigorous to mount
A horse a woman or a muse with the appropriate skill;
Like Theseus not concerned merely to live, and to have
                              lived,
But to leave a hero's mark, a palace, an invention, an
                              example,
To carry the defiance of Time a little beyond Death.

Paestum

and two books: sonnet for Jane Martindale

The Antiquities of Magna Graecia,
1807, folio . . .
Tanned like its binding, but ephemera,
We paperbacks of tourists slowly flow
In bizarre clothes and stunned by the intense
August sun through Paestum, languidly,
Stained-glass-light on the plates of that immense
Solidity and diuternity . . .
And *Poets in a Landscape.* These were dead –
Horace, Juvenal, Propertius,
And Vergil, who knew this Greek city well –
Half a millennium nearer to us,
Though their less stable groups of molecule
Have all been long since redistributed.

Corfu

To have brought our two sons for a while
    To this asphodel island
Nausicaa described to her undressy
    Though courteous guest –
'We are non-starters in the usual policy
    Of interference and murder; remote in this sea
We practise what the Gods like, – horticulture,
    The arts, seamanship, – and repay our good
                              fortune' –
Is to see them as out-of-date and misplaced princes,
    Properer sons for King Alcinous.
Dear lads, if only you were heirs of his realm
    And palace, this climate and those fellows
Among whom the blind poet, eating apart, is sent
    The king's vintage and the best cut off the joint . . .
How can I ship such gentles on
    And not myself turn into a stone man,
Like the men who shipped the hero to Ithaca,
    Dumping them on a fouled shore to fight and trick it
                              out?
Here by the Korakian we seem legitimate. Anywhere else
    One needs to be a hero like Odysseus
Even to claim one's own palace.
    But possibly each of them is.

Norfolk

I *Rippon*

Today passing Rippon Hall with its tall chimneys
And rooks and white park cattle – only at Woodbastwick
And Bawdeswell are similar herds – recalled an October
Shooting party there many years ago.
We had stopped to eat blackberries when we heard horses
And the three Miss Birkbecks arrived, riding back to the
house,
Talkative, sunlit, beautiful, all on grey horses.
Those moments, had a painter been there, might have
lasted generations,
Time and bad luck framed out, for others to recall
That now-long-vanished morning as we look back
Into moments framed out of time in Tuscany or Holland;
Or a great poet might have kept them beautiful
Three thousand years and more, as Homer has kept Helen
With blood in her cheek and a full breast and bright eye.
Today nothing – not the rooks in the air – appeared even
to have moved.

But only these lines, essentially, are left.

II *Oxnead*

On Lady Katherine Paston's Tomb

Sun set three hundred years,
These marble shadows on the wall still stand,
Fixed by her husband's grief, and Stone's hand,
Long vanished skill, and wealth, and tears.

Outside her dilapidated
Church the usual June again transposes
The graveyard offals into grass and roses,
Beauty and corruption equated,

Balanced principles,
Whereby this white *memento-mori* is
Now mere *memoria pulchritudinis,*
New summer dappling her walls.

We're not the tomorrow, alas,
Of this lady's wish; her treasures scattered for ever,
Her mansion now green mounds beside the river,
Not a Paston left to wear her flesh . . .

And since we put the resurrection
Even of annual crops to chance,
Eternity of blood's no longer, as once,
Any man's confident possession.

We do with less than that:
The uncertain hope that someone not yet born
May saunter here on a remote June morning
To find the key under the mat.

III *Felbrigg*

R.W.K-C.

Families have no beginning, but can end,
Though 350 armigerous years
Brighten the vellum. But life may descend
Obliquely, and a score of Norfolk squires
Are summed up here into a fresh dimension
That can progenerate outside the reach
Of county gossip and outlive the plantation
Of these long woods of Spanish chestnut and beech.
The rooks come idling home. The piled clouds glow
And fade this late October afternoon.
Here in his great library, ill and slow,
He leans between his lamp and the young moon,
Become the elements of more than nature.

IV *Dilham*
De L'Election de son Sepulcre

To end here, in this region,
Long seemed appropriate
To one who has made of it
    Almost religion.

But now, near death and less
Illusioned, now mine's been
(And must) a part, a scene
    Of unsuccess – ?

Ostensibly, all's well.
The city I still love
(Am proud to be native of
    And provincial)

Thrives, orderly, well-planned;
And round it, still, some rare
Country houses where
    More than the land

Is farmed, quiet halls and manors
That have, in metaphor,
Stood two millennia
    As lamp-bearers –

Places Xenophon
Or Horace would have recognized,
Or Ronsard, as civilized,
    Or Addison . . .

(As Barton and Hoveton are,
And Bixley; and, further from home,
Somerleyton and Raveningham
    And Westacre).

But the heart it is
Dies first, man's and the State's.
Hand, province articulates,
    While metropolis,

Thrombotic, stiff, infected
With late-Roman disease –
As in my despairing fifties
    I am infected,

Whom the years did not redeem,
And who himself brought no one
And nothing to redemption
    In all his time.

It's Spring. The warmth and rain
Re-energise corn and cattle.
Goth, Sassanid and Vandal
    Furbish again

Their sparkling frontiers.
And the psychoses here
Cyclically recur.
    Strange, all these years

(And shameful) that have ticked
Me almost to eternity
Never physicked my world, or me,
    Or metaphysicked.

The zeitgeist can't, like nature,
Turn its own corpse to grass.
The dying culture has
    No certain reculture.

One's appropriate heritage
Would seem a refugee's,
Among mined-out resources,
    And rusty age.

So, the clock is set
For some one else's turn.
I can't teach, or learn,
    What's not learnt yet,

Nor have heart left to try,
Since hope, and strength, and care
Have failed to solve the affair
    Of Now and I.

On the Limitations of Art

Artists do no more
Than interrupt time a little,
Though they use blood itself to colour
Verse, palette or score;

Engrave no rule, uncover
No mystery, merely save
His exploit for the hero,
His dream for the mystic or the lover,

Or even this autumn day –
Dear family of joy, and of grief –
For a while, for a little delay,
Till the record's a dead leaf.

Like the heart of Robert Bruce
Our treasure, though we case it in gold,
Travels only a short way
On the journey to Jerusalem.

500 copies of this book have been
printed on Basingwerk Parchment. Of these,
30 have been signed by the authors.